D0010703

Dɪꜱɴᴇʏ PRESENTS A PIXAR

THE INCREDIBLES
MEET THE BOYS

Ladybird

THE INCREDIBLES – MEET THE BOYS

Mr Incredible

With the power of Super strength, Mr Incredible was once the world's greatest Super – his secret identity is Bob Parr.

Dash

Mr Incredible's eldest son is called Dash – he is the Super boy with Super speed.

Jack-Jack

Mr Incredible's baby boy's Super powers are yet to be determined.

Frozone

Frozone is Mr Incredible's best friend and quite literally the world's coolest Super. His secret identity is Lucius Best.

Syndrome

An evil villain with a truly diabolical plan.

BOB PARR...
husband, father

Bob has a wife
and three children
and works for
an insurance
company named
Insuricare. To
most people,
he would
appear to be
an ordinary
man with an
ordinary life...

But things are far
from ordinary for
Bob and his family.
He was once
Mr Incredible,
fighting evil and
saving the world.

Normal life does not
suit Bob. He wishes
he could put on his
Super suit and live as
a hero again.

Bored by civilian day-to-day living, Bob goes out with his friend Lucius and listens to a police scanner for any signs of trouble where they can anonymously jump in and save the day.

After losing his job for accidentally pushing his boss through a few walls (he still has his Super strength), Bob is mysteriously called upon for a new, top-secret mission... Mr Incredible is back!

MR INCREDIBLE... is back

Mr Incredible is recruited by Mirage and sent on a mission to Nomanisan. There he has to defeat the Omnidroid, a learning robot that is out of control. Mr Incredible manages to disable the robot with his Super powers.

Some time later, Mirage calls Mr Incredible for another assignment. When he arrives at the conference room on Nomanisan to learn about his mission, he is surprised by a bigger, stronger Omnidroid.

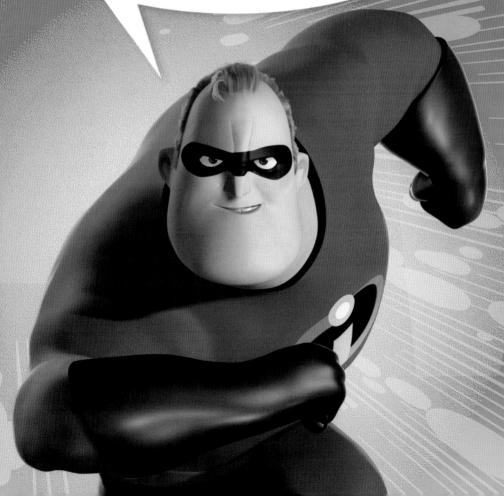

The Omnidroid has been invented by Syndrome, once Mr Incredible's biggest fan – now his biggest enemy! Luckily for Mr Incredible, his family of Supers sets out to help him!

EVERY SUPER HAS A SECRET IDENTITY. I DON'T KNOW A SINGLE ONE WHO DOESN'T. WHO WANTS THE PRESSURE OF BEING SUPER ALL THE TIME?

MR INCREDIBLE'S JOKES

What do you call Mr Incredible covered in minestrone?
A soupy-hero.

What do you call a Super with something in his eye?
Mr Blinkcredible!

Who's stronger than ten ordinary men and perfectly round?
Mr Incrediball.

What seafood does Mr Incredible like best?
Mussels.

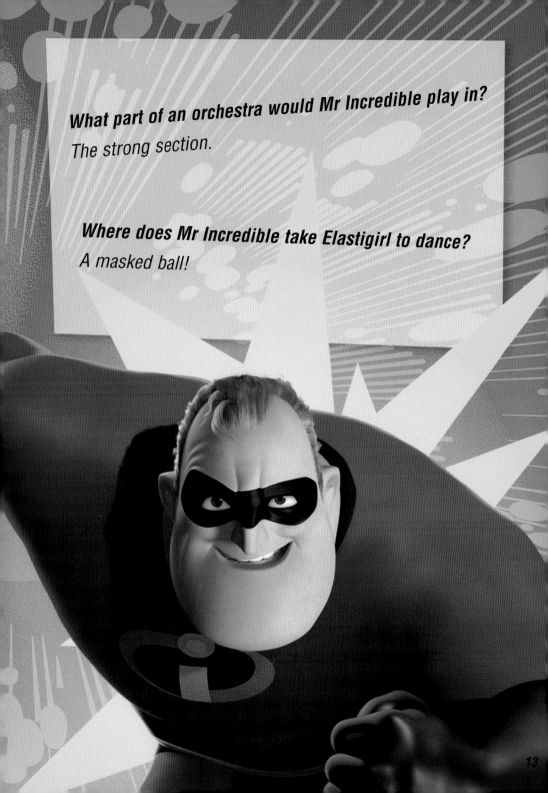

What part of an orchestra would Mr Incredible play in?
The strong section.

Where does Mr Incredible take Elastigirl to dance?
A masked ball!

DASH AND JACK-JACK...
ordinary kids?

Dashiell Parr, otherwise known as Dash, is ten years old. Like most boys his age, he has lots of energy, enjoys showing off to his friends and playing pranks at school.

Dash has the power of Super speed and he has trouble hiding it. Luckily, he's never been caught.

Dash gets tired of being told to act "normal" by his parents and doesn't see why he should hide his powers. Dash doesn't see the point of having Super powers if he can't even show them off!

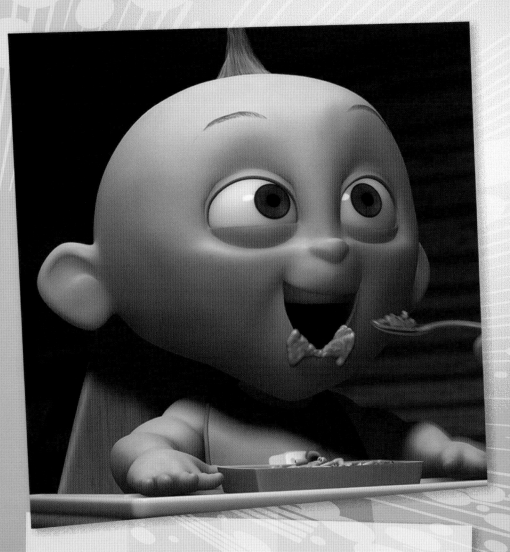

Jack-Jack is the youngest member of the Parr family. He loves to watch the incredible chaos that's caused when his elder brother and sister argue. He thinks it is great fun! Almost two years old, all he really does is talk nonsense and throw food around.

Just like any ordinary baby. (Or is he… ?)

DASH AND JACK-JACK...
the boy Supers

Dash loves it when he finally gets to wear his Super suit. He can run as fast as he likes and help beat the bad guys! (But he knows that when the Super suit and mask come off, then it's back to being normal.)

He uses his Super speed to escape from Syndrome's guards and then to help save the city.

DASH IS MY NAME. SPEED IS MY GAME.

Jack-Jack hasn't shown any powers yet, but Edna Mode designs him a Super suit anyway. Little does Syndrome know that there's more to this tiny toddler than meets the eye. After all Super powers do run in his family.

DASH AND JACK-JACK'S JOKES

What should you give Jack-Jack when he's behaving like a little monster?
Plenty of room.

Why is Dash like a snotty nose?

'cos he won't stop running.

What runs in the Parr family?
Dash.

What has four legs, barks and can run fast?
A Dashhound.

What do you call an Incredible in a hurry?
Dash.

What are Dash's favourite vegetables?
Runner beans

FROZONE...
cool as ice

In the heyday of the Supers, Frozone was quite literally the coolest Super on the planet.

He has the ability to create sheets of ice from the moisture in the air. He can then slide along them with his special boots, looking hip and cool as he does so.

Frozone's undercover identity is Lucius Best, he is Bob's best friend. Unlike Bob, he's not overly keen to relive his Super days. In fact he's quite happy with his ordinary non-Super life. But whenever Bob needs help, Lucius will always be there.

When the Omnidroid attacks the city, Frozone pulls out his old Super suit and joins the fight. He takes on the destructive robot with Mr Incredible, Elastigirl and the kids. Will their combined Super strengths be enough to defeat Syndrome and his Omnidroid?

WE ARE TALKING ABOUT THE GREATER GOOD.

FROZONE'S JOKES

What does Frozone like to do in the evenings?
Just chill out.

What's Frozone's favourite food?
Chilli.

What do you call a scuba-diving, ultra-cool Super?
Deep Frozone.

What's Frozone's favourite dessert?
Frozone yoghurt!

What's Frozone's favourite part of a supermarket?
The Frozone food counter.

How does Frozone make fairy cakes really cool?
He covers them in icing.

What was Frozone doing in the classroom?
Being a coolteacher.

SYNDROME...
evil genius

Syndrome (formerly known as Buddy) was once Mr Incredible's biggest fan. As a boy, Buddy wanted nothing more than to be a Super just like his hero. Buddy wanted to work with Mr Incredible so much that he even offered his services as Mr Incredible's sidekick, complete with costume and rocket boots!

In fact, Buddy proclaimed himself Incrediboy. But Mr Incredible told Buddy he worked alone. Rejected by his hero, Buddy became bitter and wanted revenge. He became Syndrome!

Now, as Syndrome, he comes up with an evil plan. He builds a robotic weapon – the Omnidroid. The Omnidroid is an intelligent robot that can learn how to fight its opponents. He tests his invention on Supers, killing them off in the process.

Syndrome's idea is that if he sets the Omnidroid loose and then saves the city from the robot, everyone will treat him as a hero. Fortunately, there is a family of real Supers to stop him.

SYNDROME'S JOKES

Why did Buddy make Mr Incredible-shaped pastry cases?

He was starting a flan club.

What does it say on the Omnidroid's tombstone?
Rust In Peace.

What do you call a villain in a washing machine?

Spindrome.

Which robotic fighting machine just doesn't work?

The Omnidud.

What do you call Mr Incredible's arch enemy on a diet?

Slimdrome.

What do you get if you cross Syndrome with a tiny beetle?

A weevil genius.

MR INCREDIBLE'S TIPS

NEVER UNDERESTIMATE YOUR FRIENDS AND FAMILY - YOU NEVER KNOW WHEN YOU MIGHT NEED THEM TO GET YOU OUT OF TROUBLE!

KEEPING FIT IS A BIG PART OF BEING A SUPER. BUT YOU DON'T NEED TO BE A SUPER TO BE SUPER FIT. GET OUT YOUR BIKE, RUNNING SHOES OR SWIM SUIT AND GET EXERCISING!

I USED TO WORK ALONE, BUT AFTER THIS INCREDIBLE ADVENTURE I'VE REALISED THAT IT'S GREAT TO WORK IN A TEAM!

YOU DON'T HAVE TO BE A SUPER TO BE SPECIAL. EVERYONE IS SPECIAL IN THEIR OWN WAY.

Published by Ladybird Books Ltd
A Penguin Company
Penguin Books Ltd, 80 Strand, London, WC2R 0RL, England
Penguin Books Australia Ltd, Camberwell, Victoria, Australia
Penguin Group (NZ), cnr Airborne and Rosedale Roads, Albany, Auckland 1310, New Zealand

Copyright © 2004 Disney Enterprises Inc./Pixar Animation Studios

The term OMNIDROID used by permission of Lucasfilm Ltd.

All rights reserved

3 5 7 9 10 8 6 4 2

Ladybird and the device of a ladybird are trademarks of Ladybird Books Ltd

Manufactured in Italy

www.ladybird.co.uk